L'ANGLAIS POUR LES ENFANTS

READ ENGLISH WITH ZIGZAG -3

Copyright © 2022 Zigzag English / Lydia Winter

All rights reserved. No part of this publication may be reproduced or transmitted in any form without the written permission of the author.

ISBN: 978-1-914911-10-1

www.zigzagenglish.co.uk

www.zigzagenglish.co.uk – BOOKS FOR ENGLISH LEARNERS
OUR BOOKS FOR CHILDREN

Our bilingual picture books for younger children. *Funny stories in simple, useful everyday English, with colour photos.*
English with Tony -1- Tony moves house
English with Tony -2- Tony is happy
English with Tony -3- Tony's Christmas
English with Tony -4- Tony's holiday
My best friend

Our coursebook for beginners *(age 7 to 11)*
English for Children - 1st Coursebook *(Essential vocabulary and grammar for beginners)*

Our dialogue books for beginners *(age 7 to 11).*
I Speak English Too! - 1
I Speak English Too! - 2

Our series of reading and comprehension books for beginners *(age 7 to 11).*
Read English with Zigzag - 1
Read English with Zigzag - 2
Read English with Zigzag - 3
   Audiobook at Audible.com

Our vocabulary book with photos, word puzzles and more *(age 7+)*
300+ mots en anglais / 300+ englische Wörter / 300+ palabras en inglés / 300+ parole inglesi

The Learn English Activity Book for Children *(A1 - A2, elementary). (Recommended for children in early secondary school.)*

Our series of reading and comprehension books for children at elementary level *(A1 - A2) (recommended for ages 10 to 13). With lots of language activities.*
Read English with Ben - 1
Read English with Ben - 2
Read English with Ben - 3

Our YOU DECIDE adventure book with 1 beginning and 19 endings. A2
(11+)   Your Bilingual Fairy Tale Adventure

Our series of reading and discussion books about a family with superpowers (with writing tasks) for children at secondary school, A2 - B1
I Live in a Castle – Book 1 – My Superpower
I Live in a Castle – Book 2 – The New Me

The Speak English, Read English, Write English Activity Books – 3 books from A1 to B2, for older children and adults.

Our non-fiction book with language activities
Learn English with Fun Facts! – A2 - B2

English Dialogues for Teenagers – for ages 11 to 17, A2 - B2

OUR BOOKS FOR ADULTS

Our 3 Grammar books with grammar-focused dialogues
Learn English Grammar through Conversation – A1, A2 and B1

Our Dialogue books for adults (with vocabulary lists and comprehension questions). Audiobooks are available for some of these books – at Audible.com.
50 very Easy Everyday English Dialogues (A2)
50 Easy Everyday English Dialogues (A2 - B1)
50 Intermediate Everyday English Dialogues (B1 - B2)
50 more Intermediate Everyday English Dialogues (B1 - B2)
40 Advanced Everyday English Dialogues (B2 - C1)
40 Intermediate Business English Dialogues (B1 - B2)
40 Advanced Business English Dialogues (B2 - C1)

Our activity books for adults and older children
The Speak English, Read English, Write English Activity Books – 3 books, for A1 - A2, A2 - B1 and B1 - B2.

Our non-fiction book with language activities
Learn English with Fun Facts! – A2 - B2

Contents

    Les objectifs de cette série de livres: 5
    Comment utiliser cette série de livres: 5
    Quoi d'autre? Et après? 5
1 I'm not a cat 7
2 One or two things you need to know 8
3 Dogs are better than cats 9
4 Big, bigger, biggest 10
5 A long time ago 11
6 Old enough 13
7 A very brave thing 15
8 At school 18
9 Something interesting 19
10 Goldilocks and the 3 bears 21
11 Cat in a tree 24
12 Terrible danger 26
13 Dogs can't climb trees 29
14 The school rules 31
15 The plan 33
16 Lunch 35
17 A lazy cat 37
18 Animal tracks 38
19 Bad dog! 39
Find the opposites. 42
What are the words? 42
    Réponses: 43
    Merci d'avoir lu ce livre! 45
    From: I Speak English Too! - 2 46
    From: Read English with Ben - 1 47
    From: The Learn English Activity Book 48

Les objectifs de cette série de livres:

1. Proposer une lecture amusante et drôle.
2. Donner à votre enfant la confiance nécessaire pour lire en anglais.
3. Enseigner à votre enfant des mots et des phrases clés. Les livres les présentent, les répètent et les développent petit à petit, afin d'élargir la compréhension de votre enfant.
4. Aider votre enfant à apprendre la grammaire anglaise essentielle de manière ludique.

Comment utiliser cette série de livres:

1. Votre enfant pourra peut-être h lire les livres tout seul. C'est très bien! Mais si vous parlez anglais, vous pouvez l'aider à améliorer sa prononciation en l'encourageant à lire à haute voix. **Les livres 1 et 2 sont également disponibles en livre audio.**
2. Il y a des listes de vocabulaire, pour aider votre enfant à comprendre le texte et à apprendre de nouveaux mots.
3. Il y a des questions de compréhension, dont les réponses se trouvent à la fin de chaque livre.
4. Il y a des activités linguistiques pour aider votre enfant à enrichir son vocabulaire et sa grammaire.

Quoi d'autre? Et après?

1. Notre série de dialogues simples - **I Speak English Too!** - est conçue pour les parents qui souhaitent aider leur enfant à commencer à parler anglais. Elle est idéale pour 1 parent et 1 enfant, ou pour 2 enfants. Elle commence par les bases, en présentant et en développant des mots et des phrases clés pour aider votre enfant à faire des progrès rapides. En quelques leçons, votre enfant pourra avoir de petites conversations en anglais avec vous.
2. Lire des livres (très simples) en anglais fait une grande différence. Nous vous recommandons également de regarder des séries télévisées simples pour enfants, même si elles sont conçues pour les enfants de langue maternelle anglaise qui sont un peu plus jeunes que votre enfant. Les livres audio sont également excellents, surtout juste avant d'aller se coucher (ce qui aide l'enfant à retenir la nouvelle langue). Ne vous attendez pas à ce que votre enfant comprenne tout tout de suite - les livres audio peuvent être écoutés à plusieurs reprises, et votre enfant comprendra mieux à chaque fois.

From wolf to pet

1 I'm not a cat

Oh, look at all those children. Hello, children! I'm your friend! Can I **wash** your **face** for you? Is that okay? Can we go for a walk? Can I take my ball? Can you **throw** the ball for me?

What's that? What did you say?

I'm not Zigzag, no. I'm not a cat. I'm not a tiger. Do I look like a cat or a tiger?

No, I don't. I look like a dog. That's because I AM A DOG.

I'm a beautiful, big, black and white dog. I'm white with black spots. I'm a dalmatian dog.

Do you know my name? Do you remember who I am?

That's right. I'm Pam!

Vocabulary:
- to wash   laver
- face   visage
- to throw   jeter

2 One or two things you need to know

If you have a dog:

1. You have to take your dog for a walk every morning.

2. You have to take your dog for a walk every evening.

3. Do NOT **forget** to take your dog for a walk!

Vocabulary:
- to forget   oublier

3 Dogs are better than cats

I'm Pam. I'm not Zigzag, I'm Pam.

Sorry about that.

No, I'm not sorry. I'm not sorry - I'm **happy**. I'm happy, because - guess what? I'm **better** than Zigzag.

I'm a dog, and Zigzag is a cat. Zigzag is NOT A TIGER. He's a cat.

Dogs are better than cats. So - I'm better than Zigzag. **Right?**

I'm bigger than Zigzag. I'm nicer than Zigzag. I'm more beautiful than Zigzag. I'm more intelligent than Zigzag. I like children more than Zigzag does.

And this is my book. It's not Zigzag's book - it's mine!

Vocabulary:
- happy   heureux, content
- better   meilleur
- right?   pas vrai?

4 Big, bigger, biggest

This is a small dog. It's not very big. It's the smallest dog.

This is a bigger dog. It's quite big.

This dog is even bigger. It's the biggest dog. It's really very big. It's enormous.

5 A long time ago

Some dogs are big and some dogs are small. Some dogs have long **ears** and some dogs have short **tails**. Some dogs are brown and some dogs are white with black spots **like** me.

Some dogs...

Okay, you know what I mean. All dogs are different.

But a very, very, very, very, very long time ago, all dogs were the same. That's right - all dogs were:

WOLVES!!

Wolves are enormous. Wolves have **sharp teeth**. Wolves are really scary. But most of all, wolves are **BRAVE**.

A long time ago, I was a wolf. Now, I'm a dog and I live in Adam and Poppy's house with Zigzag the cat.

But I'm still brave.

Vocabulary:
- a long time ago — il y a longtemps
- ear — oreille
- tail — queue
- like — comme
- wolf — loup
- sharp — pointu
- tooth — dent
- brave — courageux

6 Old enough

Adam is four years **younger** than Poppy. When Adam was a **baby**, Poppy was **already** at school. When Adam **learned** to talk, Poppy learned to read. When Adam learned to walk, Poppy learned to run races.

Then Adam went to nursery with the other very small children and **painted** pictures with his hands. And Poppy started to **write stories**.

But now, **at last**, Adam's old enough to go to school with Poppy.

On his first day at school, Adam was excited. He really wanted to go to school. He didn't want to be little. He wanted to be a big boy.

He walked to school with Mum and with Poppy and her best friend Jessica. He wore his **own** school uniform – black trousers and a red top. He had his own red book bag. He **felt proud**. He felt a little bit scared.

Questions:
1. How much older than Adam is Poppy?
2. How did Adam feel about starting school?
3. Why was his book bag red?

Vocabulary:
- younger   plus jeune
- baby   bébé
- already   déjà
- to learn   apprendre

- to paint   peindre
- to write   écrire
- story   histoire
- at last   enfin
- own   propre
- to feel   se sentir
- proud   fier

7 A very brave thing

This summer, I did a very brave thing. I did the bravest thing a dog can do.

We all went for a picnic. Well, not Zigzag, because he's a cat. Cats have to stay at home.

There was a river. Mum and Dad and Poppy and I can swim. But Adam can't swim. He's too young.

Adam was in danger. Mum and Dad and Poppy were there. But they didn't **see** the danger.

I saw the danger. I saw Adam run and fall into the water. I jumped into the water. It was **deep**. It was too deep for me.

I swam to Adam. He put his arms round my **neck**. I **pulled** him out of the water.

Everyone said "Good dog! Brave dog!"

I'm a big, strong, brave dog and I **saved** Adam.

Vocabulary:
- to see   voir
- deep   profond

- arm   bras
- neck   cou
- to pull   tirer
- to save   sauver

8 At school

At school, there were so many children. There were hundreds of them. **Nearly all** of them were older and bigger than Adam. Because it was Adam's first day, Mum was there. She took a photo of Adam in front of the school. And then she went into the classroom with Adam. Adam wanted Mum to stay with him. He started to **cry**. But Mum said goodbye, and she **left**.

Adam looked at all the other boys and girls in his class. There were lots and lots of them. He **only** knew one of them. Billy, from nursery. Adam didn't like Billy, and Billy didn't like Adam. "Hello, Billy," said Adam. Billy said **nothing**.

Adam sat on the **floor** with all the other children. The teacher told a story. It was the story of Goldilocks and the Three Bears.

Questions:
  1. *Why did mum go into the classroom with Adam?*
  2. *Was Adam happy to be at school?*
  3. *Why didn't Billy talk to Adam?*

Vocabulary:
- nearly — presque
- all — tous
- to cry — pleurer
- to leave — partir
- only — seulement
- nothing — rien
- floor — plancher

9 Something interesting

Adam went to school today. It was very quiet here without him.

Mum and dad were **out**. Poppy and Adam were at school. Only Zigzag was here. I like Zigzag, but he's **just** a cat. He doesn't understand much. He went to school with Poppy once, but I don't think he learned **anything**.

I went into the garden. I watched Zigzag **catch** a spider. I watched Zigzag eat the spider. Zigzag said it was delicious. I looked for a spider, but I couldn't find one.

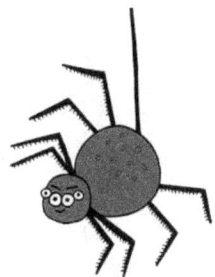

Then I saw something interesting. Something very interesting. The next door neighbour's white cat was in the next door neighbour's garden.

I did a bad thing. I knew it was a bad thing, but I did it.

I **barked** at the cat – WOOF WOOF! Then I jumped over the **fence** into the next door neighbour's garden. The cat ran. I chased her. I chased her round and round the garden and up the neighbour's tree. She sat in the tree and looked at me.

Vocabulary:
- out   sorti
- he is just…   il n'est qu'un…
- he didn't learn anything   il n'a rien appris
- to catch   attraper
- to bark   aboyer
- fence   clôture

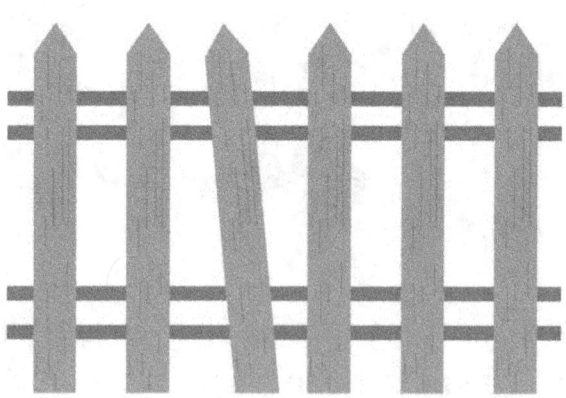

10 Goldilocks and the 3 bears

Goldilocks was a girl with **gold** hair (really?) who went into the **forest**, looking for some breakfast.

She found it in a bears' house (do bears live in houses?) and ate it.

Luckily for Goldilocks, the bears were out. Bears are extremely big and strong and sometimes eat little girls.

Then Goldilocks sat on a little chair and **broke** it.

She was tired, so she went upstairs to the bedroom and went to sleep on Baby Bear's bed.

When the three bears got **back** home, they were hungry. They wanted to eat their breakfast, but it was gone. Baby Bear wanted to sit on his chair, but it was broken. When they found Goldilocks on Baby Bear's bed, Father Bear wanted to eat her, but Baby Bear wanted to play with her.

Goldilocks **woke up**. She was scared. She jumped out of the window and ran home. She never went into the forest again.

Questions:
1. *Why did Goldilocks go into the forest?*
2. *Were the bears at home?*
3. *Did Baby Bear want to eat Goldilocks?*

Vocabulary:
- gold — d'or
- forest — forêt
- to break — casser
- to get back — revenir, rentrer
- to wake up — se réveiller

11 Cat in a tree

The white cat sat in the tree. It sat in the tree for five long minutes.

I wanted that cat. I don't know why I wanted her, but I did.

Zigzag is a cat, and I don't chase Zigzag. But Zigzag is family. I chase every other cat. All dogs chase cats. It's what we do.

But I had a problem. Cats can **climb** trees. Dogs can't climb trees. The white cat was in a tree. I needed to go **up**, or I needed the cat to come **down**.

I tried to climb the tree. I really, really **tried**. But it was no good. I'm big, strong, brave and intelligent, but I can't climb.

I **asked** the cat to come down. I said I wanted to talk to her. I was very **polite**. She was polite too, but she said no. She didn't want to come down. She was comfortable in the tree. It was nice up there.

I wanted that cat.

Vocabulary:
- to climb   grimper
- to go up   monter
- to come down   descendre
- to try   essayer
- to ask   demander
- polite   poli

12 Terrible danger

Adam **listened** to the story, but he didn't like it. It was scary.

The teacher showed the children a picture of Goldilocks. She was a very small girl. Then the teacher showed them a picture of the three bears. Baby Bear was quite cute, but Mother Bear was enormous and Father Bear was the biggest bear **ever**.

Adam knew Goldilocks was in terrible danger. **If** the bears came home and found Goldilocks in their house, they would probably eat her. If she tried to run away, they would chase her and catch her. **Then** they would eat her.

When the teacher read that Goldilocks climbed onto Baby Bear's bed and went to sleep, Adam **jumped up** and **shouted**: "Don't go to sleep, Goldilocks! **Run away**! The bears are coming!" The teacher looked at Adam and told him to sit down and be quiet.

Father Bear didn't eat Goldilocks. But he very nearly did, thought Adam.

Questions:
1. *Which bear was the biggest?*
2. *What did Baby Bear look like?*
3. *What was the most dangerous thing Goldilocks did?*

Vocabulary:

- to listen — écouter
- the biggest ever — le plus gros du monde
- if — si
- then — puis
- to jump up — se lever (vite)
- to shout — crier
- to run away — s'enfuir

13 Dogs can't climb trees

Do you know what I decided to do?

Dogs can't climb trees. That was the problem. Dogs can't climb trees, but cats can. So the white cat was in the tree, and I was under the tree. The cat was safe. Or was she?

It was simple, really.

Most cats are my enemies. But one is my friend. That's right – Zigzag is my friend, my family.

I jumped back over the fence into my garden and looked for Zigzag. He was where he **usually** is. He was on the sofa in the living room, sleeping.

I bit his tail just a little bit, to wake him up. He wasn't happy. He **hissed** at me.

I **explained** my problem with the white cat.

"Please help me, Zigzag," I said.

"Okay," said Zigzag. "But only if you **give** me what I want".

Maybe he's more intelligent than I thought.

Vocabulary:
- most   la plupart
- usually   habituellement
- to hiss   siffler
- to explain   expliquer
- to give   donner

14 The school rules

After the story, Adam's class went into the school **hall** - the biggest room in the school. All the other children in the school were already there, sitting on the floor.

The Headteacher **welcomed** the new children in Adam's class to the school. Then everyone **stood up** and sang a **song**. Adam didn't **know** what to sing, but he tried to **copy** the others.

After that, the Headteacher read the school **rules**:
1. Get to school on time.
2. Listen to the teacher.
3. Put your hand up if you want to ask a question.
4. Always **try hard**.
5. Don't **waste time**.
6. Be **kind** and polite.

Adam was **worried**. He wanted to ask a question, but he was too scared to put his hand up.

If a child broke a rule, was there a **punishment**?

Questions:
1. *What was the biggest room in the school called?*
2. *Which school rule do you think is the most important?*
3. *If you break a school rule at your school, is there a punishment?*

Vocabulary:
- hall — salle
- to welcome — accueillir
- to stand up — se lever
- song — chanson
- to know — savoir
- to copy — copier
- rule — règle
- to try hard — faire un effort
- to waste time — perdre du temps
- kind — gentil
- worried — inquiet
- punishment — punition

15 The plan

This was the plan. It wasn't **difficult**. In fact, I thought it was very easy.

Zigzag is much bigger than the white cat. He just had to climb the tree and chase the white cat down to me. Simple.

But first, I had to do something for Zigzag.

Poor Zigzag. Because he's just a cat, he can't do much. He can't open the kitchen door. He can't open the fridge door. He can't take the cat food out of the fridge.

Zigzag hates waiting for dinner time. So he **often** asks me to give him his cat food. I **always** say no. Zigzag eats too much. **More** food isn't good for him.

But I really, really wanted that white cat. So, just this **once**, I opened the kitchen door and opened the fridge door. I took the cat food out of the fridge.

Zigzag ate some cat food. "I'm tired now," he said. "I want to go to sleep on my sofa".

"Oh no." I said. "Now you have to do what *I* want. Climb that tree!"

Vocabulary:
- difficult   difficile
- often   souvent
- always   toujours
- more   plus de
- once   une fois

16 Lunch

Adam was hungry. When he went to nursery, he had a snack at eleven o'clock every morning. Today, he had to wait **until** lunchtime at half past twelve.

He played with **sand** and water and balls. He painted a picture of his cat and dog. He looked at the picture books in the big bookcase. He tried to write his name with a **pencil**.

And at last it was lunchtime. Some children had **packed lunches** from home in beautiful lunchboxes. They ate their sandwiches outside in the **playground.** But Adam went to the big hall again. This time, it was **full** of tables and chairs. He **queued** up for his food and sat down at a table next to a boy from his class. Lunch was chicken with **mashed potato** and **peas**. With strawberry ice cream for pudding. It wasn't delicious, but it wasn't too bad.

After lunch, Adam and his new friend ran outside. Adam saw Poppy playing football with the **older** boys and girls. He started to **enjoy** school.

Questions:
1. What was the most fun thing that Adam did?
2. What do you think of Adam's school lunch? Was it like your school lunches?

Vocabulary:
- until — jusqu'à
- sand — sable
- pencil — crayon
- packed lunch — panier repas
- lunchbox — boîte à lunch
- playground — cour de récréation
- full of — rempli de
- to queue — faire la queue
- mashed potato — purée de pommes de terre
- pea — petit pois
- older — plus âgé
- to enjoy — aimer, apprécier

17 A lazy cat

Zigzag wasn't happy. He's a lazy cat. To be honest, he's an extremely lazy cat. He never wants to help people. He never wants to help other animals. He only thinks about himself. It's not really his fault. He's just a cat.

He walked into the garden. Very slowly. He jumped onto the garden fence. He jumped down into the neighbour's garden. He looked up at the tree. The white cat looked down at him. She stayed exactly where she was.

Then Zigzag ran at the tree. He jumped. And he fell. He fell back down. Zigzag is a big cat. He's a fat cat. I don't think he's very good at climbing trees.

Zigzag looked at me. "You ate the cat food." I said. "Now climb the tree!" Zigzag tried again. This time he **made it**. He was in the tree. But where was the white cat?

Vocabulary:
- to make it   réussir

18 Animal tracks

Look out for animal tracks in your garden or park. You can find them in snow or mud.

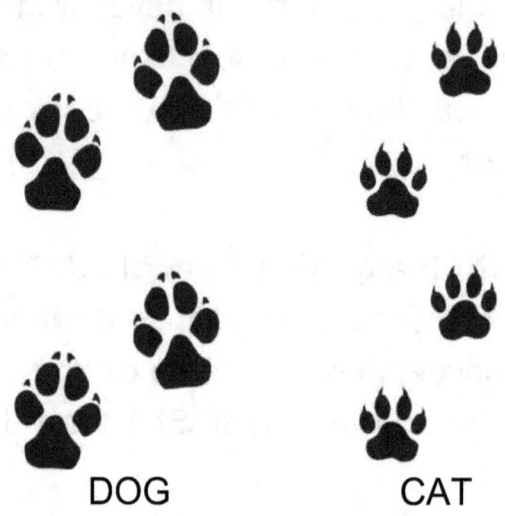

DOG   CAT

Watch out for bears – they're dangerous!

19 Bad dog!

The white cat was at the **top** of the tree. She was at the end of a thin branch.

"Go on, Zigzag! Chase that cat down!"

Zigzag slowly climbed up the tree. He climbed higher and higher. He climbed onto the white cat's branch. He was **almost** there.

CRACK!!

The branch broke. Zigzag fell down. The white cat fell down. I saw her and she saw me. She ran and I ran. I chased that cat round the garden. I chased her round the garden again. I chased her onto the **street**. I chased her down the street.

"Pam! Stop! Bad dog!"

Adam? Adam and Poppy and Mum? Back from school already? Where's the white cat? Oh no. She's up **another** tree. I WANT THAT CAT!

"Oh Pam", said Adam. "I had such a great time at school today."

Vocabulary:
- top — cime, sommet
- almost — presque
- street — rue
- another — un autre

Find the opposites.

up	go
never	in
bad	different
the same	wake up
out	noisy
stop	dangerous
quiet	down
easy	good
cute	always
safe	scary
go to sleep	difficult

What are the words?

Adam is alm-st five. He's very y-ung, but he's a pol-t- child. He al-ays says thank you.

My dad says English is quite e-sy. But I'm ter-ibl- at it!

Your English is b-t-er than my English.

Please read me the -tor- of Goldilocks and the Three Bears. – In a m-n-te!

Réponses:

6
1. She's four years older than Adam.
2. He felt excited, scared and a little bit proud. He really wanted to go to school.
3. Because his school uniform was red.

8
1. Because it was his first day at school.
2. No, he wasn't happy. He didn't want his mum to leave.
3. Because he didn't like him.

10
1. She went into the forest to find some breakfast.
2. No, they weren't; they were out.
3. No, he didn't want to eat her. He wanted to play with her.

12
1. Father Bear was the biggest.
2. He looked quite cute.
3. The most dangerous thing she did was to go to sleep on Baby Bear's bed.

14
1. It was called the school hall.
2. You decide.

16
1. You decide.
2. You decide.

up	down
never	always
bad	good
the same	different
out	in
stop	go
quiet	noisy
easy	difficult
cute	scary
safe	dangerous
go to sleep	wake up

Adam is almost five. He's very young, but he's a polite child. He always says thank you.

My dad says English is quite easy. But I'm terrible at it!

Your English is better than my English.

Please read me the story of Goldilocks and the Three Bears. – In a minute!

Merci d'avoir lu ce livre!

Si vous avez des questions ou des suggestions pour améliorer le livre, vous pouvez m'envoyer un courriel à l'adresse suivante: lydiawinter.zigzagenglish@gmail.com.
Les suggestions pour de nouveaux livres sont toujours les bienvenues.

Vous trouverez le site web de Zigzag English ici:
www.zigzagenglish.co.uk.
Votre enfant et vous pouvez découvrir nos autres livres pour enfants et adultes, lire le blog et faire d'autres activités en anglais.

N'hésitez pas à laisser un avis pour ce livre. Merci beaucoup!

Dans les pages suivantes, vous trouverez des extraits d'autres livres destinés aux enfants de niveau débutant à élémentaire.

From: I Speak English Too! - 2

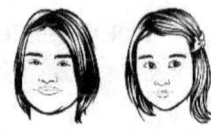

8A: A week's holiday

Katie: It's my **half term** holiday next week. A **whole** week with no school!

Anna: Are you going **away**?

Katie: Yes. We're going to the Lake District.

Anna: What's that? Where is it?

Katie: It's in the **north** of England. There are lots of **mountains** and **lakes**. It's very beautiful.

Anna: Lucky you! I have school next week.

Katie: School is really hard at the moment. I'm tired. I need a **break**.

Anna: Is your whole family going?

Katie: No. My mum has to work next week. So she's **staying** at home.

Anna: Your **poor** mum.

From: Read English with Ben - 1

14. Present

The day after the last day of school was the first day of the summer holidays. But Ben didn't feel excited. He felt unhappy.

He **lay** on his bed in his bedroom with a book. But he didn't read the book. He thought about all those years at primary school. He thought about his friends.

His mum **called** him. "It's lunchtime, Ben! Come downstairs!"

Ben **sighed**. He went downstairs to the dining room. He **started** to say: "I'm not hungry, mum. I don't want any lunch." But then he stopped. What was that on the table? It was a **parcel.** Was it a **present**? For him?

From: The Learn English Activity Book for Children

CATEGORIES

WRITE DOWN 3:

1. School subjects
2. Small pets
3. Nice things to eat
4. Languages
5. Books in English
6. Annoying things children in your class do
7. Sea animals
8. English songs
9. Plants
10. Horrible things to eat
11. Funny people
12. Nice things to do on holiday
13. Jobs you don't want to do when you grow up
14. Long English words
15. Sports
16. Vegetables
17. Things your parents can do that you can't do
18. Short English words
19. Countries
20. American movies

www.ingramcontent.com/pod-product-compliance
Lightning Source LLC
LaVergne TN
LVHW020443080526
838202LV00055B/5330